The
Little Way
for Every Day

The Little Way for Every Day

Thoughts from Thérèse of Lisieux

St. Thérèse of Lisieux

Selected and translated by
Francis Broome, CSP

Paulist Press
New York/Mahwah, N.J.

Nihil Obstat: Arthur J. Scanlon, STD, *Censor Liborum*

Imprimatur: + Patrick Cardinal Hayes, Archbishop, New York

New York, September 11, 1931

The *Imprimatur* is the Church's declaration that a work is free from error in matters of faith and morals, but does not imply that the Church endorses the contents of the work.

Cover design by Trudi Gershenov
Book design by Lynn Else

Library of Congress Cataloging-in-Publication Data

Thérèse, de Lisieux, Saint, 1873–1897.
   [Sainte Thérèse de l'Enfant Jesus. English. Selections]
   The little way for everyday : thoughts from Thérèse of Lisieux / St. Thérèse of Lisieux; selected and translated by Francis Broome.
      p. cm.
   ISBN 0-8091-4374-7 (alk. paper)
   1. Christian life—Catholic authors. 2. Devotional calendars—Catholic Church. I. Broome, Francis. II. Title.
   BX2350.3.T48213 2006
   242′.2—dc22

                             2005026710

Published by Paulist Press
997 Macarthur Boulevard
Mahwah, New Jersey 07430

www.paulistpress.com

Printed and bound in the United States of America

Contents

Note from the Translator

The work *Sainte Thérèse de l'Enfant Jesus* from which these thoughts are taken consists of the autobiography of the Little Flower, extracts from her poems and letters, and excerpts from the evidence submitted for her canonization. It is by far the most authentic record of her life and teaching.

—Rev. Francis Broome, CSP

January

In this is love,
not that we loved God
but that he loved us
and sent his Son to be the
atoning sacrifice for our sins.
(1 John 4:10)

1

When Christ said, "Give me to drink,"[1] it was the love of His poor creatures that He, the Creator of all things, desired. He thirsted for love.

2

Birthday of St. Thérèse, January 2, 1873
Because I was little and feeble, Our Lord stooped down to me and lovingly instructed me in the secrets of His love.

3

How good our Jesus is. How loving and tender. How easy it is to touch His heart.

4

Jesus does not consider time[2] since He is eternal. He considers only love.

5

Jesus does not need books or learned men to instruct souls. He, the Doctor of doctors, teaches without noise of words.[3] I have never heard Him speak, but I know that He is within me.

6

Feast of the Epiphany

With Your little hand that caresses Mary, You sustain the universe and bestow life; and You think of me, O Jesus, my little King.

7

Jesus does not reveal everything to souls at one time. He usually gives His light only gradually.

8

It seems to me, O Jesus, that if You find souls offering themselves as victims to Your love, you will rapidly consume them; You will never again hold back from them the flames of infinite tenderness that have their source in You.

9

Though You have the seraphim in Your heavenly court, You still seek my love; You desire my heart. Jesus, I give it to You.

10

St. Thérèse takes the habit of Carmel,
January 10, 1889.

In one word—I wish to amuse the little Jesus and to give myself over to His baby caprices.

11

There is only one who can understand love, and that is our Jesus. He alone can give us infinitely more than we can ever give Him.

12

On this earth, where everything changes, one thing alone does not change—the conduct of the King of heaven toward His friends.

13

I believe that it is Jesus Himself, hidden at the bottom of my poor little heart, who acts in me in some mysterious way and tells me everything He wishes me to do at the present moment.

14

Yes, I have believed for a long time that the Lord is more tender than a mother, and I have known more than one maternal heart.

15

Jesus more and more desires a throne of gold, and this throne is your pure heart.

16

Through all my life, the Lord has been pleased to surround me with love; my first recollections are of smiles and tender caresses.

17

What sweet joy to think that the Lord is just, that He takes into account our weakness, and knows perfectly the frailty of our nature.

18

O my God, You are love.[4]

19

I see that the Lord alone is immutable, that He alone can fulfill my immense desires.

20

Do not fear. If you are faithful in pleasing Jesus in little things, He will be obliged to help you in the greater things.

21

Feast of St. Agnes

At any price I wish to gain the palm of St. Agnes;[5] if not by blood, it must be done by love.

22

O Jesus, I want to be magnetized by Your divine glance. I want to become the prey of Your love.

23

O my God, You have surpassed even my desires, and I would tell of Your mercies.

24

Yes, all my hopes will be fulfilled. The Lord will work wonders in me that will surpass even my great desires.

25

To be just means not only to deal severely with the guilty; it means to recognize good intentions and to repay virtues. I hope as much from the justice of the good God as I hope from His mercy.

26

To pick up a pin for love can convert a soul. It is Jesus alone who can give such value to our actions. Let us then love Him with all our heart.

27

The more You wish to give us, O God, the more You make us desire.

28

I so want to be a saint, but I feel my weakness, and so I beg You, O my God, to be my sanctity.

29

Feast of St. Francis de Sales

Yes, all is well when we seek only the Divine Pleasure.

30

We should look for no support except in Jesus. He alone is immutable. What joy to think that He can never change.

31

Yes, Jesus is content with even a glance or sigh of love.

February

We love because he first loved us.
(1 John 4:19)

1

I wish so much to love Jesus—to love Him as He has never yet been loved.

2

Feast of the Purification

O, how I love the Blessed Virgin. If I were a priest, how often would I speak of her. She is described as unapproachable, whereas she should be pointed to as a model. She is more of a mother than a queen.

3

If we fall, all is atoned for by an act of love, and Jesus smiles.

4

You know that our Lord does not look at the greatness or the difficulty of an action but at the love with which you do it. What then have you to fear?

5

My soul sighs for Your beautiful heaven, that I may love You—love You ever more and more.

6

O Jesus, You know that it is not for the reward that I serve You, but simply because I love You and in order to save souls.

7

I do not think there will be a judgment for victims of Divine Love. Rather the good God will hasten to repay with eternal delights His *own* love that He will see burning in their hearts.

8

Why are you afraid to offer yourself as a victim to the Merciful Love? If you offered yourself to the Divine Justice, you might fear, but Love will have compassion on your weakness and will treat you with sweetness and mercy.

9

Do not be afraid to tell Jesus that you love Him—even if you don't feel that you love Him. That is the way to force Him to aid you.

10

You know, O my God, that I have but today on this earth to love You.

11

Feast of Our Lady of Lourdes

I do not tremble when I see my weakness, for the treasures of a mother belong also to her child, and I am your child, O dear Mother Mary.

12

I do not desire sensible love. If it is sensible to Jesus, that is enough for me.

13

"You must try to sleep," the infirmarian told St. Thérèse. Thérèse answered, "I cannot, my sister. I suffer too much—but then I pray." "What do you say to Jesus?" asked the infirmarian. "I don't say anything. I love Him."

14

How sweet is the way of love. Yes, one may fall or commit infidelities; but love, knowing how to draw profit from everything, quickly consumes whatever could displease Jesus, leaving at the bottom of the heart only a humble and profound peace.

15

One phase of heaven causes my heart to beat faster—the love that I shall receive and that I shall be able to give.

16

Jesus, Jesus, if it is so sweet to desire love, what shall it be to possess it, to enjoy it for all eternity?

17

O Jesus, my Love, at last I have found my vocation. My vocation is to love. In the heart of my Mother the Church, I will be the love.

18

By love and not by fear, does a soul avoid committing the least voluntary fault.

19

My heaven was to love God, and I felt, in my ardor, that nothing could tear me away from this Divine Object that had taken me captive.

20

Jesus does not need our deeds, but He does need our love.

21

I have heard it said at retreats and elsewhere that an innocent soul never loves God as much as a repentant soul. Well, I want to prove that this is wrong.

22

As I grew older, I loved the good God more and more, and very often I offered Him my heart.

23

Now my only desire is to love Jesus unto folly. Yes, it is love alone that attracts me.

24

For those who love Him, and who, after each little fault, come throw themselves into His arms and ask pardon, Jesus thrills with joy.

25

My dear Savior, repose on my heart. It belongs to You.

26

Yes, we must keep everything for Jesus with a jealous solicitude. It is so good to work for Him alone.

27

O burning Dart of Love, consume me without cease; wound my heart while I am still on this earth. Divine Jesus, realize my dream to die of love for You.

28

I understand that without love, all deeds, even the most brilliant, are as nothing.

29

It shall not be said that a woman of the world does more for her merely human spouse than I do for my beloved Jesus.

March

*Let us run with perseverance the race
that is set before us, looking to Jesus the
pioneer and perfecter of our faith,
who for the sake of the joy that was set
before him endured the cross,
disregarding its shame.*
(Heb 12:1b–2b)

1

Jesus wishes to bring His kingdom to souls more by suffering and persecution than by brilliant preaching.

2

Trials help greatly to detach us from earth. They make us look to God, rather than to this world.

3

The martyrdom of the heart is no less fruitful than the shedding of blood.

4

It is so consoling to think that Jesus, Divine Strength Itself, has experienced our weakness, that He trembled at the sight of the bitter chalice,[6] the chalice that He had so ardently desired.

5

My joy is to love suffering. I smile in the midst of tears and receive with thanksgiving the thorns as well as the flowers.

6

Jesus has always treated me like a favorite child. It is true that His cross has accompanied me from my childhood, but He has made me love this cross passionately.

7

I do not fear trials sent by Jesus, for even in the most bitter suffering we can see that it is His loving hand that causes it.

8

Willingly would I remain all my religious life in this dark tunnel of spiritual dryness into which

Jesus has led me. I wish only that my darkness may obtain light for sinners.

9

Do you know what days are my Sundays and feast days? They are the days when the good God tries me the most.

10

Nothing is too great to suffer in order to win the palm of eternal life.

11

I value sacrifice more than ecstasy. I find my happiness in suffering, as I find it nowhere else.

12

Jesus gives to me just what I can bear at each moment, no more;[7] and if a moment later He increases my suffering, He also increases my strength.

13

"You have had many trials today," someone said to St. Thérèse. "Yes, but I love them," she answered. "I love everything that the dear God gives to me."

14

If I did not suffer from moment to moment, I would not be able to keep patience, but I see only the present moment; I forget the past and take care not to peer into the future.

15

The good God has always helped me. He has aided me and led me by the hand from my childhood. I depend on Him. My sufferings may reach their limit, but I am certain that He will never abandon me.

16

All that I have written about my desire to suffer is true. I am not sorry that I have surrendered myself to love.

17

Jesus wants to take complete possession of your heart. That is why He makes you suffer much, but O what joy will fill your soul at the happy moment of your entrance into heaven.

18

I have reached the point where I cannot suffer because all suffering has become sweet to me.

19

I have not an insensible heart, and it is just because it can suffer much that I want to give Jesus all that this heart can endure.

20

Suffering united with love is the one thing we should desire in this valley of tears.

21

For what can give greater joy than to suffer for Your love? The more intense the suffering, and the more it is hidden from the eyes of creatures, the more does it cause You to smile, O my God.

22

How merciful is the way by which the Divine Master has always led me. He has never made me wish for anything without giving it to me; that is why His bitter chalice seems delightful to me.

23

If it pleases the good God, I willingly consent to have my life of bodily and spiritual sufferings prolonged for years. No, I do not fear a long life; I do not refuse the combat.

24

My heart beat violently when I pressed my lips to the dust of the Colosseum, that dust purpled by the blood of the first Christians. I asked the grace to be a martyr also for Jesus, and I feel at the bottom of my heart that I was heard.

25

Feast of the Annunciation
I should rather simply confess, "The Mighty One has done great things for me,"[8] and the greatest of these is to have shown me my littleness, my incapability of all good.

26

I tell Jesus that I am glad not to be able to see, with the eyes of my soul, this beautiful heaven that awaits me, in order that He may vouchsafe to open it forever to poor unbelievers.

27

As I visited the terrible prisons at Venice [at the Palace of the Doges], I was carried back in spirit to the times of the martyrs. I would joyfully have chosen this dark dungeon as my dwelling rather than deny my faith.

28

O my God, I choose everything. I do not want to be a saint by halves. I am not afraid to suffer for You.

29

What happiness to suffer for Him who loves us even unto folly. What happiness to be counted as fools in the eyes of the world.

30

O Guardian Angel, fly in my stead to those who are dear to me; dry their tears; tell them of the goodness of Jesus and of the benefit of suffering, and O so softly, murmur my name.

31

You should voyage on the stormy sea of life with the abandonment and love of a child who knows that its father loves it and will not forsake it in the hour of danger.

April

"So I tell you, whatever you ask for in prayer, believe that you have received it and it will be yours."
(Mark 11:24)

1

What offends Jesus, what wounds His Sacred Heart, is lack of confidence in Him.

2

Confidence and nothing else is what leads us to love.

3

I wish to suffer everything that my Beloved wishes. I wish to allow Him to do with His little ball whatever He desires.

4

What pleases Jesus is to see me love my lowliness and poverty; to see the blind hope I have in His mercy.

5

My gifts are all too unworthy and so I should offer You my very soul, O most loving Savior.

6

Abandonment alone guides me. I have no other compass.

7

The only happiness here below is to strive to be always content with what Jesus gives us.

8

St. Thérèse enters Carmel, April 8, 1888.
Suffering has held out its arms to me since my entrance into Carmel, and I have embraced it lovingly.

9

My one desire is the glory of Christ. I have abandoned to Him my own glory and if He seems to forget me—well, He is free to do so, since I do not belong to myself but to Him.

10

I am sick now and will not be cured. Always I remain in peace; for a long time I have not belonged to myself but I am given over totally to Jesus. He is free to do with me whatever He wishes.

11

No, I am not an angel of heaven, but if I fall every moment of my life, I shall get up and come to You. Give me the grace that I may live by love.

12

I accept everything for the love of the good God—even the strangest thoughts that enter my mind.

13

To be truly a victim of love, we must give ourselves up entirely; for we are only consumed by love in the degree that we give ourselves to love.

14

When, with a truly filial confidence, we cast our faults into the consuming furnace of love, they will, for certain, be entirely consumed.

15

We can never have too much confidence in the good God who is so powerful and so merciful. We obtain from Him as much as we hope for.

16

Feast of St. Benedict Joseph Labre

I do not wish creatures to have one atom of my love. I wish to give all to Jesus since He has shown me that He alone is perfect happiness.

17

Yes, I wish always to depend on the abundance of heavenly gifts, knowing that everything comes from above.

18

I do not more desire to die than to live. If the Lord offered me the choice, I would choose nothing. I wish only what He wishes. I love what gives pleasure to Him.

19

O, if souls, who are as feeble and imperfect as I, could feel as I feel, no one would despair of attaining the summit of the Mountain of Love; for Jesus does not ask great deeds, but only self-surrender and gratitude.

20

Jesus deigned to show me the one way leading to this Divine Furnace of Love. This way is the self-surrender of a little child who sleeps without fear in the arms of its father.

21

O Jesus, my Divine Spouse, grant that my baptismal robe may never be stained; take me from this life rather than that I should sully my soul by committing the slightest voluntary fault.

22

O Jesus, I feel that, if by an impossibility You could find a soul weaker than mine, You would fill it with even greater graces, provided that such a soul abandoned itself with absolute confidence to Your infinite mercy.

23

I can demand nothing with fervor, except the perfect accomplishment of God's will in my soul.

24

I try to be no longer concerned about myself, and what Jesus deigns to do in my soul I leave unreservedly to Him.

25

Since I belong to Jesus as His little plaything, to console Him and give Him pleasure, I should not oblige Him to do my will instead of His own.

26

O my God, I wish to console You for the ingratitude of wicked men, and I beg You to take away from me the liberty to displease You.

27

O my Beloved, I offer myself to You, that You may perfectly accomplish in me Your holy designs, and I will not allow anything created to be an obstacle in their path.

28

Feast of St. Paul of the Cross

When we are expecting nothing but suffering, we are quite surprised at the least joy; but then suffering itself becomes the greatest of joys when we seek it as a precious treasure.

29

Beatification of St. Thérèse, April 29, 1923
I will spend my heaven doing good upon earth.
This is not impossible, since the angels, though
always enjoying the beatific vision, watch over
us. No, I cannot be at rest until the end of the
world.

30

I fear only one thing—to keep my own will;
take it, my God, for I choose all that You
choose.

May

For she is a reflection of eternal light,
a spotless mirror of the working of God,
and an image of his goodness.
(Wis 7:26)

1

My dear Mother Mary, I think that I am more happy than you. I have you as a Mother and you haven't the Blessed Virgin to love as I have.

2

My heart sighs for You, O Jesus. My one desire is to possess You, my God.

3

O how large my heart seems when I compare it with the goods of this world, since altogether they cannot satisfy it. But when I compare it with Jesus, how small it seems.

4

To keep the word of Jesus[9] is the one condition of our happiness, the proof of our love for Him. And this Word is Himself since He is called the *Logos* or *Uncreated Word of the Father.*[10]

5

Christ wishes that I love Him because He has forgiven me, not much, but all.[11]

6

Let us love, since that is all our hearts were made for.

7

I imagine my soul as a piece of waste ground, and I ask the Blessed Virgin to take away from it all the rubbish, that is, all the imperfections.

8

St. Thérèse makes her First Communion,
May 8, 1884.
I love You, my Jesus, and I give myself to You forever.

9

I do not wish to be troubled with passing things. My Beloved will take the place of all these. I wish to walk in the groves of His love, where no one can intrude.

10

O sparkling nature, if I did not see God in you, you would be naught but a great tomb.

11

Jesus, You are the star that leads me on; You know that Your dear face is my heaven here below.

12

In heaven I shall live amid joy since all trial will be gone forever, but here below I must live by love.

13

Then I cried that willingly would I be plunged into hell, that place of torments and blasphemies, in order that God be loved there forever. This could not bring Him glory, but when we love, we are bound to say many foolish things.

14

If, by an impossibility, the good God Himself did not see my good deeds, I would not be grieved. I love Him so much that I wish to give Him pleasure, even without Him knowing that it is I.

15

I, the little spouse of Jesus, love Jesus for Himself.

16

O Jesus, may I one day die of Your love.

17

Canonization of St. Thérèse, May 17, 1925
I have never given to the good God anything but love; He will return that love. After my death I will let fall a shower of roses.

18

Jesus helps us without seeming to do so, and the tears that sinners make Him shed are dried by our poor feeble love.

19

A soul in the state of grace has no fear of the demons who are cowards—ready to flee before the glance of a child.

20

I know that love strengthens every vocation, that love is everything, that it embraces all times and all places, because it is eternal.

21

I am so convinced that love is the only thing capable of making us pleasing to the good God that this love is the one treasure I desire.

22

To live by love is to imitate Mary Magdalene, bathing Your feet with tears and perfume, kissing them lovingly, and drying them with her beautiful hair.[12]

23

Our Beloved does not need our brilliant deeds nor our beautiful thoughts. If He wanted sublime concepts, has He not the angels, who surpass in knowledge the greatest geniuses of the world?

24

It is so sweet to call the good God "Our Father."

25

Yes, in spite of my littleness, I am not afraid to gaze at the Divine Sun of Love, and I long to approach Him.

26

O my God, truly "Love is only repaid by Love."[13] Therefore I have sought and found the only way to solace my heart—by returning You love for love.

27

The good God has given me a heart so faithful, that when it has once loved, it loves forever.

28

You alone can satisfy my soul, O Jesus, for I must love You for all eternity.

29

I know only one thing—to love You, O Jesus.

30

You ask how to obtain perfection. I know but one way—love.

31

Feast of the Blessed Virgin,
Mother of Fair Love

O Virgin Mary, change my heart into a beautiful pure corporal, to receive that white Host in which our sweet Lamb hides Himself.

June

*The cup of blessing that we bless, is it not
a sharing in the blood of Christ?
The bread that we break, is it not a
sharing in the body of Christ?*
(1 Cor 10:16)

1

How little known is the great and merciful love
of the heart of Jesus. The fact is that to enjoy
this treasure we must be humble and recognize
our nothingness, and that is just what many
people will not do.

2

Give me a thousand hearts that I may love You;
but even these are not enough, O Supreme
Beauty. In order that I may love You, give me
Your Sacred Heart Itself.

3

Remember that the dear Jesus is there in the tabernacle expressly for you, for you alone. Remember that He is consumed with a desire to come into your heart.

4

O how I love Jesus, who comes in the Host to unite Himself to my enraptured soul.

5

Since this second visit of our Lord, to receive Him was my one desire. This was allowed me on all the great feasts, but alas, how far apart did these feasts seem to me.

6

Your love has gone before me since my baby-hood. It grew as I grew and now it is an abyss whose depths I cannot plumb.

7

O my Divine Savior, I can sleep on Your heart, for it belongs to me.

8

I especially liked processions of the Blessed Sacrament. What a joy to strew flowers in front of the good God. But before letting them fall to the ground, I threw them as high as I could, and I was never so happy as when I saw one of my rose petals touch the sacred monstrance.

9

St. Thérèse offers herself as a victim of Divine Love, June 9, 1895.
I besought Jesus to draw me into the flames of His love and to unite me so closely to Himself that He might live and act in me.

10

For my sake You live hidden in the Host; for Your sake I too wish to be hidden, O Jesus.

11

For a long time Jesus and [I] had looked at each other and understood. The day of my First Communion, our meeting could not be called a mere glance; it was a fusion.

12

O Jesus, the golden ciborium that You desire, above all others, is myself.

13

Keep my heart pure, shield me with Your presence, just for today.

14

How much benefit have I received from the beauties of nature, bestowed in such abundance. How they raise me to Him who placed such wonders in this land of exile that is to last only a day.

15

I only desire to receive Your dear glance, O Jesus. I wish to smile always, resting on Your heart.

16

You know well that my one martyrdom is Your love, O Sacred Heart of Jesus.

17

I cannot receive Holy Communion as often as I wish, but O Lord—are you not all powerful? Remain in my heart as in the tabernacle and never leave Your little victim.

18

Yes, Jesus wishes to make a palace in your heart.

19

It is wrong to spend one's time in useless worries, instead of reposing on the heart of Jesus.

20

When the enemy troubles me, I behave like a soldier. Knowing that it is cowardly to fight a duel, I turn my back upon the enemy. Then I turn to my Jesus and tell Him that I am ready to shed every drop of my blood to confess that heaven really exists.

21

My heaven is hidden in the tiny Host where Jesus my Spouse veils Himself for love of me.

22

Only self-surrender can place me in Your arms, O Jesus. It is this virtue that makes me feed on the Bread of Love reserved for Your chosen ones.

23

When the demon succeeds in keeping a soul from Communion, he has gained everything and Jesus weeps.

24

I wish to smile, resting on Your heart, and there tell You again and again that I love You, O my Lord.

25

Your heart, which preserves my innocence, could not disappoint my confidence. In You O Lord I place my hope that after this exile I shall see You in heaven.

26

If through feebleness I sometimes fall, may Your divine glance purify my soul, consuming all my imperfections, like the fire that transforms everything into itself.

27

You are my peace, my happiness, my only love, O Jesus.

28

To live by love is to banish all fear, all remembrance of past faults.

29
Feast of Saints Peter and Paul

If St. Peter had said to Jesus, "Lord, give me the courage to follow You to death," I am certain that this courage would not have been refused him.

30

I know that my heart is too weak to be an apostle, but Jesus, do lend me Your heart.

July

Giving thanks to the Father who has...
rescued us from the power of darkness and
transferred us into the kingdom
of his beloved Son, in whom we have
redemption, the forgiveness of sins.
(Col 1:12–14)

1
Feast of the Precious Blood
I resolved to remain continually, in spirit, at the foot of the cross, to receive the sacred drops of Blood and then to apply them to souls.

2
I pour out the Blood of Jesus on souls and then I offer to Jesus these same souls refreshed by the Blood of Calvary.

3

It is not to remain in the golden ciborium that Jesus comes down from heaven each day, but that He may find another heaven—the heaven of our souls.

4

How can a heart given over to human affection unite itself closely to God? I am sure that it is not possible.

5

Since the age of three I have refused the good God nothing. But I do not glory in this. Do you see how the setting sun gilds the treetops? Well, my soul appears to you all shining and illumined because it is exposed to the rays of love.

6

To love Jesus and make Him loved. How sublime that is.

7

In realizing that I could do nothing of myself, my task [as mistress of novices] became simplified. I strove only to unite myself more and more to God, knowing that the rest will be added to me.[14]

8

I wish that Jesus would take over my faculties so that I would never perform actions that were human and personal but actions that were divine,[15] inspired and directed by the Spirit of Love.

9

It is my weakness that gives me all my strength.

10

Everything will be for Jesus—yes, everything—and even when I have nothing to offer, I shall give Him this nothing.

11

You know, O my God, that I have never wished for anything but to love You alone. I desire no other glory than this.

12

I am glad to follow my Spouse for Himself, and not for His gifts. He is so beautiful, so entrancing—even when He is silent and hides Himself from me.

13

You know, O my God, that my only desire is to make You loved and one day to die a martyr of Your love.

14

I have another great desire—to love only the good God, and to find no joy save in Him.

15

If you wish to be a saint, it is not hard. Have one aim—to please Jesus and to unite yourself more intimately to Him.

16

I beg you not to remain any longer at the feet of Jesus but to follow that first impulse that would carry you into His arms.

17

We cannot say as did Pilate, "What is truth?"[16] Truth we possess, since the beloved Jesus dwells in our hearts.

18

Feast of St. Camillus

You should consider yourself as a little slave whom everyone has a right to command.

19

Prayer is a cry of gratitude and love, in the midst of trial as well as in joy.

20

To me, prayer is a lifting up of the heart; it is a glance thrown toward heaven.

21

Prayer is anything that elevates, anything supernatural that enlarges the soul and unites it to God.

22

Feast of St. Mary Magdalene

When I see Magdalene wash with her tears the feet of the Master,[17] whom she meets for the first time, I feel that her heart understood the abyss of love and mercy in the heart of Jesus.

23

A learned man once said, "Give me a fulcrum and a lever and I will lift the world." The saints have obtained what Archimedes could never obtain. The Almighty has given them a fulcrum—Himself, Himself alone; for a lever they have prayer.

24

It is in loving You, O Jesus, that I attain to the Father;[18] my poor heart keeps Him forever; O Holy Trinity, You are the prisoner of my love.

25

Jesus wishes to receive charity from us like a poor man. He places Himself, as it were, at our mercy. He wishes to take nothing from us unless we give it freely, and our least gift is precious in His sight.

26

Just as the sun lights the great cedar and the tiny flower, so does the Divine Radiance illumine each individual soul, whether great or lowly.

27

To live by love is to go through life sowing peace and joy in hearts.

28

Jesus deigns to look only at the little virtues we offer to Him, and these virtues give Him consolation.

29

When we see how wretched we are we should not keep looking at ourselves, but should look on our Well-Beloved Jesus.

30

I have always been satisfied with what the good God has given to me—even with the gifts that seemed less good or beautiful than those of others.

31

God has no need of anyone to carry out His work of sanctification, but just as He allows a skillful gardener to raise rare and delicate plants, so does He wish to be aided in sanctifying souls.

August

"Blessed are the poor in spirit, for theirs is the kingdom of heaven. Blessed are the meek, for they will inherit the earth."
(Matt 5:3, 5)

1

He who on this earth chooses to be the poorest and the most unknown for the love of our Lord, in heaven will be the first, the noblest, and the richest.

2

It is enough if we desire to be victims of love, but we must be willing to remain poor and weak—and that is the difficulty.

3

While on this earth, we must be attached to nothing, not even to the most innocent things, for they will fail us when we least expect it.

4

The only place not liable to envy is the last place.[19] In this last place there is no vanity nor affliction of spirit.

5

I know that Jesus would rather see you stumbling along by night over a rocky path, than in daylight over a path covered with flowers, because the flowers might hold you back.

6

Believe me—to write books of piety, to compose sublime poems, all this is not worth as much as the smallest act of renunciation.

7

Make to the good God the sacrifice of never gathering the fruit—that is, to feel all your life a repugnance to suffering and humiliation, to see the flowers of your desires and good will fall to the ground without producing anything.

8

Only that which is eternal can satisfy us.

9

May I always seek and find You, my God. May creatures be nothing to me, and I nothing to them.

10

I will love God alone and will not have the misfortune of attaching myself to creatures, now that my heart perceives what He has in store for those who love Him.

11

Jesus made me understand that the only true glory is that which shall last forever.

12

To love Jesus, to be His victim of love—the more weak and wretched we are, the more fitted we are for the operations of this consuming and transforming love.

13

The remembrance of my faults humbles me and makes me afraid to reply on my own strength, which is nothing but weakness.

14

Let us avoid all display; let us love our lowliness; let us be affected by nothing. Then we shall be poor in spirit and Jesus will come to seek us.

15

Jesus made me understand that only in obedience was I pleasing to Him.

16

It is so sweet to serve the good God in darkness and in trial, for we have only this life to live by faith.

17

If you are nothing, do you forget that Jesus is everything? You have only to lose your nothingness in His infinity and think only of loving Him.

18

Yes, even if I had on my conscience every possible crime, I should lose none of my confidence; my heart breaking with sorrow, I should go and throw myself into the arms of my Savior.

19

When we commit a fault, we should never attribute it to a physical cause such as sickness or the weather, but we should confess that this fall was due to our lack of perfection—though without ever getting discouraged.

20

It is enough to humble ourselves, to bear patiently our imperfections. There lies true sanctity for us.

21

"When I think how much I have to acquire!" said a sister to St. Thérèse. "Say rather 'to lose,'" Thérèse answered, "for Jesus has charge of filling your soul with virtues as fast as you will get rid of the imperfections."

22

O let us profit by the short moment of life. Let us give pleasure to Jesus; let us save souls for Him by our sacrifices. Above all, let us be lowly—so lowly that the world can tread us under foot without us appearing to notice it.

23

This is the way with our Lord: He gives as God, but He wishes us to be humble of heart.[20]

24

O, I wish to become very lowly, so that Jesus can rest His head on my heart, and there He may know that He is loved and understood.

25

Let us humbly range ourselves among the imperfect; let us estimate ourselves as little souls whom the good God must sustain every instant.

26

I know from experience that the only happiness on earth consists in being hidden and in absolute ignorance of created things.

27

I know that the more rapidly one advances on the way of perfection, the further one considers one's self from the goal.

28

Feast of St. Augustine

You love St. Augustine and St. Mary Magdalene, whom much was forgiven because they loved much.[21] I also love them. I love their repentance and above all their loving audacity.

29

I beseech You, my Divine Jesus, to send me a humiliation every time I try to place myself above others.

30

He whose kingdom is not of this world[22] has shown me that the only desirable royalty consists in wishing to be ignored and counted as nothing.

31

Even when the fire of love seems dead, I still throw little straws upon the embers, and I am certain that the fire will be rekindled.

September

The commandment we have from him is this: those who love God must love their brothers and sisters also.
(1 John 4:21)

1

The principal plenary indulgence, and one that anybody can gain without the usual conditions, is the indulgence of charity, which covers a multitude of sins.[23]

2

Nothing is sweeter than to think well of one's neighbor.

3

I seek little happenings, nothings, to give pleasure to my Jesus: for example, a smile, a kind word, when I would rather be silent or show no interest.

4
Now I see that true charity consists in bearing with all the faults of our neighbors, in not being surprised at their weaknesses, in being edified at their least virtues.

5
The good God will do everything I wish in heaven, because I have never followed my own will on earth.

6
To die of love is a very beautiful martyrdom. It is the one that I wish to suffer.

7
It is God's will that, while on this earth, souls should share their heavenly gifts by prayer, so that when they reach their home in heaven, they can love each other with a grateful love, with an affection higher than that of the most perfect human family.

8
Nothing renders community life more unhappy than unevenness of disposition.

9

In giving itself to God, the heart loses none of its natural tenderness. On the contrary, this tenderness increases as it becomes more and more divine.

10

Yes, I love my family very much. I cannot understand saints who did not love their families.

11

The death of love that I desire is the death of Jesus on the cross.

12

Let us work together for the salvation of souls. We have only the day of this life to save souls and to give them to the Lord as proofs of our love.

13

It is such a joy to help Jesus save souls that He has purchased with His Blood, for they are only waiting for our help to stop them from falling into the abyss.

14

We have only the short moments of this life to work for God's glory. The devil knows this, and that is why he tries to make us waste time in useless things.

15

I wish to give my Beloved to drink. I feel myself consumed with thirst for souls and I wish at any price to snatch sinners from the eternal flames.

16

In spite of my littleness I can give to God my most tender affection.

17

Your Love is my martyrdom. The more I feel it burn within me, the more I desire You. Jesus, grant that I may die of love for You.

18

One word or a pleasing smile is often enough to raise up a saddened and wounded soul.

19

Yes, it is the Lord, it is Jesus, who will judge me; and to make His judgment favorable, or rather not to be judged at all, since He said, "Do not judge, and you will not be judged."[24] I wish always to think charitably of others.

20
We are not bound to be justices of peace but we are bound to be angels of peace.[25]

21
O Guardian Angel, cover me with your wing; O Friend, illumine my path; direct my footsteps and be my protection—just for today.

22
O my dearest Star, yes, I am glad to feel that, in Your presence, I am lowly and frail, and thus my heart is in peace.

23
O my God, even if You did not know it, I would still be glad to suffer, hoping that by my tears, I might prevent, or atone for, a single fault against faith.

24
I cannot be downcast, since in everything that happens to me, I see the loving hand of Jesus.

25

I too have distractions, but as soon as I perceive the distraction, I pray for the persons who come into my imagination, and so they draw benefit from my distractions.

26

The most sublime inspirations are nothing without works.

27

When I am charitable, it is Jesus alone who acts through me; the more I am united to Him, the more do I love all my sisters.

28

To live by love is my heaven, my destiny.

29

Remember, O Jesus, that I entered Carmel in order to bring souls to your kingdom of heaven.

30

Death of St. Thérèse, September 30, 1897
[Her last words:] "O, I would not wish to have suffered less." [Then looking at her crucifix:] O, I LOVE HIM—MY GOD, I LOVE YOU.

October

*"Truly I tell you, whoever does not receive
the kingdom of God as a little child
will never enter it."*
(Luke 18:17)

1

I feel that my mission is only beginning; my
mission to make the good God loved as I love
Him, to give my little way to souls.

2

Feast of the Guardian Angels
O beautiful Angel Guardian, you stay with me
on this earth, enlightening me with your splen-
dor. You are become my brother, my friend, and
my consoler.

3
Feast of St. Thérèse

Someone asked St. Thérèse by what name they should pray to her when she reached heaven. "You may call me Little Thérèse," she replied.

4
Feast of St. Francis of Assisi

The poorer you are, the more Jesus will love you.

5

I am too little to do great things, but in my excess of love, I hope that Your love, O Jesus, will accept me as a victim.

6

I am so feeble, so weak, that I wish to be united forever to Divine Strength Itself.

7

I should be sad at sleeping so often during prayers and thanksgiving. Well, I am not. I recall that little children, when asleep, are just as pleasing to their parents as when they are awake.

8

Jesus seeks neither abilities nor talents here below. He made Himself "a lily of the valley,"[26] just to show us how He esteems simplicity.

9

Instead of becoming discouraged, I say to myself, "The good God does not inspire us with desires that could not be realized. Therefore, in spite of my lowliness, I can aspire to sanctity."

10

The lift that shall raise me to heaven is Your arms, O Jesus. That this may be so, I do not need to become greater. I must remain little and become even more lowly.

11

To come near to Jesus, we must be very little. O how few are the souls who aspire to be lowly and unknown.

12

To be little is to recognize one's nothingness, to expect everything from God as a little child expects everything of its father.

13

To be little is not to be discouraged at our faults, for children fall often, but they are too small to hurt themselves very much.

14

I understand that the love of our Lord reveals itself just as well in the simple soul who makes no resistance to His grace, as in the most sublime soul.

15

A long time ago I offered myself to the Infant Jesus, to be His little plaything. I asked him to use me, not as a costly toy that children can only look at, and dare not touch, but as a little ball of no worth, which He could throw on the ground, kick about, leave in a corner, or press tightly to His heart.

16

Far from resembling those beautiful saints who practiced all sorts of austerities from childhood, my penance consisted in breaking my self-will, in keeping back a sharp reply, in doing little kindnesses to those about me, but considering these deeds as nothing.

17

Ought not the good God, who is infinitely just and pardons so mercifully the Prodigal Son—ought he not be just toward me, who is always with Him?[27]

18

I have no other way to prove my love for You, O Jesus, but to throw flowers—that is, to let no sacrifice, word, or glance escape; to draw profit from the smallest deeds and to do them for love.

19

You see that I am a very little soul, who has nothing to offer to the good God but very little things.

20

Jesus, because of my very weakness, You have deigned to grant my childish requests, and You are willing to grant all my desires, though they be greater than the whole world.

21

I wish to show souls the little ways that have succeeded so well in my case, to tell them that there is only one thing to do here below. That is to cast before Jesus the flowers of little sacrifices, to captivate Him by caresses. That is how I have acted and that is why I shall be so well received in heaven.

22

In my little way there are only very ordinary things. It is necessary that, what I do, little souls may be able to do also.

23

I keep always little, having no other occupation but gathering flowers of love and sacrifice and offering them to God, in order to give Him pleasure.

24

I am too little to be condemned. Little children are not sent to hell.

25

I am only a weak and feeble child, but it is my very weakness that makes me dare to offer myself as a victim to Your love, O my Jesus.

26

If we had to do great deeds, we should have reason to be pitied. But how happy we are because Jesus lets Himself be captivated by very little things.

27

The only means of making rapid progress on the way of love is to remain always very little.

28

We must practice the little virtues. This is sometimes difficult to do, but the good God will never refuse the first grace that gives courage to conquer self.

29

I find it very easy to strive for perfection because I have found out that we must captivate Jesus through His heart.

30

"You will look down from heaven on us, won't you?" someone asked St. Thérèse. "O no, I will come down."

31

I beg You, O Jesus, to cast Your divine glance on a great number of little souls. I beg You to choose in this world a legion of little victims worthy of Your love.

November

But the souls of the righteous
are in the hand of God,
and no torment will ever
touch them....For though in the
sight of others they were
punished, their hope is full
of immortality.
(Wis 3:1, 4)

1

Feast of All Saints

It says in the catechism that death is nothing but the separation of soul and body. Well, I have no fear of a separation that will unite me forever with the good God.

2
All Souls' Day
If I go to purgatory, I will walk in the midst of the flames, like the three Hebrew children in the furnace, singing the canticle of love.[28]

3
No, it will not be death that will come for me. It will be the good God. Death is a phantom, a horrible specter, as it is represented in pictures.

4
"From ages past no one has heard, / no ear has perceived, / no eye has seen any God besides you, / who works for those who wait for him."[29] And all this will come soon—yes, very soon, if we love Jesus with all our strength.

5
No, I am not afraid of purgatory. I know that I am not even worthy to enter that place of expiation with those holy souls, but I know also that the fire of love is more sanctifying than the fire of purgatory.

6
After this exile there will be no more suffering, only heavenly peace. No more faith or hope, only peace and an ecstasy of love.

7

The tomorrow of this life will be eternity. Then Jesus will repay you a hundredfold for the joys you have sacrificed to Him.

8

Ah, how happy I should be at the moment of death if I had one soul to offer to Jesus. There would be one soul less in hell, one more soul to bless the good God for all eternity.

9

Jesus holds out His hand to us in order to receive a little love, so that on that radiant Judgment Day, this Savior may be able to greet us with the ineffable words—"Come, you that are blessed by my Father,...for I was hungry and you gave me food, I was thirsty and you gave me something to drink."[30]

10

The one thing I wish is to make others love the good God and, if I cannot do this in heaven, I am sure that I shall love this exile more than heaven itself.

11

I am not dying. I am entering into life, and all that I say to you here, I will make you understand when I am in heaven.

12

What attracts me to the kingdom of heaven is the call of our Lord, the hope of loving Him as I have so desired, and the thought that I shall be able to make Him loved by a great number of souls who will bless Him forever.

13

I am happy to die because I shall be able to help souls who are dear to me, far more than I can here below.

14

I do not intend to remain inactive in heaven. I want to work for the Church and for souls. I have asked this of God and I am certain that He will grant my request.

15

I shall desire in heaven the same thing as on earth—to love Jesus and make Him loved.

16

If you could see the angels, who from heaven are watching us fight in the arena! They only await the end of the strife to bestow on us flowers and crowns.

17

Had I not experienced it, I could not believe it, but I think I could die for very joy at the thought that soon I am to leave this earth.

18

It seems to me that resignation is needed to live. I feel nothing but joy when I think of dying.

19

Life is not sad; it is very joyous. If you say, "This exile is sad," I understand you. We are wrong to give the name "life" to something that will end; it is only to the things of heaven that we should apply this beautiful name.

20

In order to contemplate Your glory, we must pass through fire. I choose for my purgatory Your burning love, O Heart of my God.

21

I think that all missionaries are martyrs by desire and by will, and that, consequently, not one of them should go to purgatory.

22

Feast of St. Cecilia

Cecilia, lend me your sweet melodies. I want to convert souls to Jesus. Like you, I want to sacrifice my life. I want to give to Jesus my blood and my tears.

23

A sister spoke to St. Thérèse of the happiness of heaven. Thérèse interrupted her, saying: "That is not what attracts me." "What is it then?" asked the sister. "O, it is love. To love and be loved and come back to earth to make Love loved."

24

Feast of St. John of the Cross

True, I am not always faithful, but I do not get discouraged. I place myself in the arms of the Lord and He teaches me to "draw profit from everything, good or bad, that He finds in me."[31]

25

Jesus, may I die a martyr for You. Give me martyrdom of the soul or of the body. Ah, rather, give me both.

26

The good God does not need years to do His work of love in a soul. One ray from His heart can, in an instant, cause a soul to blossom forth for all eternity.

27

"In heaven you will be among the seraphim," someone said to St. Thérèse. "If that happens," she answered, "I won't imitate them when they cover themselves with their wings before the sight of God.[32] I will take care not to do that."

28

Since I have tried to be a little child I have no preparations to make for death. Jesus Himself will pay my expenses and the entrance-fee into heaven.

29

How can God purify in the flames of purgatory souls who are consumed by the fires of Divine Love?

30

If there is a mansion in heaven[33] for great souls, for the fathers of the desert, and for martyrs who were penitents, surely there is one for little children. Our place is waiting there if we love our Lord—Him and our Heavenly Father and the Spirit of Love.

December

Rejoice in the Lord always; again I will say, Rejoice...and the peace of God, which surpasses all understanding, will guard your hearts and mind in Christ Jesus.
(Phil 4:4, 7)

1

Jesus loves joyous hearts. He loves a soul that is always smiling.

2

If our sacrifices captivate Jesus, so do our joys; but our happiness must not be self-centered. We must offer to our Spouse the little joys that He sows along the way of life in order to take our hearts and lift them up to Himself.

3

The countenance is a reflection of the soul. You should always have a calm and serene countenance, like a little child who is always happy.

4

My one happiness is to love You, O Jesus.

5

Smile always here below. Jesus seems to tell you that when you smile at a sister you are smiling at His spouse and this will dry His tears.

6

When I suffer greatly, or when something painful or disagreeable happens, instead of taking it sadly, I receive it with a smile.

7

I experience great joy, not only when I *am* imperfect, but above all, when *I feel* that I am.

8

To be lowly is not to take credit for the virtues we practice, but to recognize that God places this treasure of virtue in the hands of His child, to make use of as He wishes; but it is always the treasure of the good God.

9

All the most beautiful discourses could not cause one act of love to be made without the grace that touches the heart.

10

Ah, how happy does the Lord make me. How easy and sweet it is to serve Him. He has always given me what I wished, or rather, He has made me wish for what He wanted to give me.

11

My peace consists in remaining little, and when I fall by the way, I pick myself up as quickly as possible and Jesus takes me by the hand.

12

Sometimes, when I read books that say perfection is reached only after conquering a thousand obstacles, my poor soul gets tired. I close the learned book that makes my head ache and dries up my heart.

13

When I read the scriptures, everything seems clear. A single word shows my soul an infinite vision. Perfection seems easy to me. I see that it is enough to recognize our nothingness and to abandon ourselves, like little children, into the arms of the good God.

14

St. Thérèse is declared Patroness of the Missions, equally with St. Francis Xavier, December 14, 1927.

I cannot perform brilliant works; I cannot preach the Gospel or shed my blood. But what matter? My brothers work in place of me, and I, a little child, keep very close to the royal throne. I love those who are carrying on the warfare.

15

He whose heart is ever watching[34] taught me that for a soul whose faith is as a grain of mustard seed, He works miracles, in order to strengthen this faith; but that for His intimates, for His mother,[35] he did not work miracles until He had tried their faith.

16

I count on the angels and saints that I may fly up to You with Your own wings, O Jesus, my Eagle.[36]

17

The only grace I ask, O Jesus, is never to offend You.

18

My deeds, my little sufferings, can make God loved all over the world.

19

If the great shadows come and hide the Star of Love; if I seem not to believe in anything but the existence of the night of this life—then shall be the moment of perfect joy, knowing that behind the dark clouds my beloved Sun still shines.

20

My Well-Beloved, O Beauty Supreme, You have given Yourself to me. In return, O Jesus, I love You. Make of my life one single act of love.

21

What I value, what alone I wish for, is to give pleasure to Jesus.

22

My heaven is to smile at the God I adore, when He wishes to hide in order to try my faith, to smile until He will again look down on me.

23

Ah, I know well, joy is not in the things that surround us; it dwells in the innermost soul.

24

My way is a way of trust and love. I do not understand souls who are afraid of such a tender Friend.

25
Christmas Day

O, how I wish to love Jesus, to love Him passionately, to give Him a thousand tokens of love, while I am still able.

26

The little Jesus demands only a sweet caress from you. Give Him your love.

27

O what a mystery; my feeble love can enthrall You, my Lord.

28
Feast of the Holy Innocents

O King of the Elect, my place in heaven is among the Holy Innocents. Like them, O Jesus, I will kiss your sweet face.

29

At this moment, when I am soon to appear before the good God, I realize more and more that one thing alone is necessary—to work only for Him and to do nothing purely for self or for creatures.

30

I do not count on my own merits, since I have none, but I trust in Him who is virtue and sanctity itself.

31

There is only one thing to do here below—love Jesus and save souls for Him, so that He may be more loved.

Notes

1. John 4:7
2. 2 Pet 3:8
3. *Imitation of Christ,* III, 43:3
4. 1 John 4:8, 16
5. The palm is a symbol for the glory of martyrdom.
6. Luke 22:42
7. 1 Cor 10:13
8. Luke 1:49
9. Luke 11:28
10. John 1:1
11. Luke 7:47
12. John 12:3
13. St. John of the Cross
14. Matt 6:31
15. Gal 2:20
16. John 18:38
17. Luke 7:38
18. John 14:23
19. Luke 14:10–11

20. Matt 11:29
21. Luke 7:47
22. John 18:36
23. 1 Pet 4:8
24. Luke 6:37
25. Luke 12:14
26. Song 2:1
27. Luke 15:31
28. Dan 3
29. Isa 64:4
30. Matt 25:34
31. St. John of the Cross
32. Isa 6:2
33. John 14:2
34. Song 5:2
35. John 2
36. Isa 40:31